WITH HEARTS ENTWINED

Light for Your Journey to Intimacy with God

SHARON DEMING

On Wisdom's Porch Publishing
(an imprint of Sharon Deming)

JOHNSON CITY, TN

With Hearts Entwined / Sharon Deming. -- 1st ed.
ISBN 979-8-9923455-0-6

To Jim.
You made a wide place in your life for God's plan for mine.

"Nothing in or of this world measures up to the simple pleasure of experiencing the presence of God."
~Aiden Wilson Tozer

Acknowledgments

All I had was a calling from God and no clue how to move forward. These precious servants of God came forward in God's perfect timing to show me the way.

Thank you, Andrew Wommack, founder of Charis Bible College. You and other anointed instructors opened my eyes to the revelation of the grace and goodness of God: Andrew, for your many messages on the grace of God; Greg Mohr, for your call for us to manifest Jesus; Barry Bennett, for your powerful ability to unpack the Word of God and transparency in the fight for your life; and Rick McFarland, for the simple truth about walking in the Spirit. God used each of you to transform my life.

Thank you, Mindy Kiker and Jenny Kochert. You, Flourish Writers, and the *Writer's Life Planning Guide* transformed me from an insecure coward with a calling into a bold author and mentor. You created a nourishing field of training, equipping, empowerment, and wisdom about the writing life that led to this finished book. You are God's gift to me.

Thank you, David Lee Martin, founder of the Anointed Authors program. I knew I needed to know you when I heard your message at a Flourish Writers virtual event. You gave me the tools and habits I needed to keep moving forward even when it was hard. Your prophetic wisdom banished *reluctance*. You haven't seen the last of me.

Thank you, Brad Bess and Bryce Bess, my pastors and friends. You believed in me and took me seriously before I did.

And thank you, Holy Spirit. Your constant direction and guidance brought my wild wanderings into purposeful steps. Your living revelation of the Word brought my aha moments into a clear message of intimacy with God.

CONTENTS

Introduction

God's inviting his church to come deeper into intimacy with him. He's calling his children by name, one by one. He's calling you. You see differences between what others seem to have with God and what you do. Maybe you believe God's promises but rarely experience them. Perhaps others live at a level of joy you wish you could experience. My hunch is wherever you are with the Lord now, it doesn't feel like enough.

God's Invitation to Intimacy

That's where I was when I saw this scripture in Isaiah. It made me very hungry for the next level of intimacy with God.

*For this reason the Lord is still waiting to <u>show his favor</u> to you so he <u>can show you his marvelous love</u>. He waits to be <u>gracious to you</u>. He sits on his throne ready to <u>show mercy to you</u>. For YAHWEH is the Lord of justice, **<u>faithful to keep his promises</u>**. **Overwhelmed***

> *with bliss* are <u>all</u> who will **<u>entwine their hearts</u> in
> him**, *waiting for him to help them. (Isaiah 30:18 TPT;
> my emphasis added here and all verses following)*

What an invitation the word *entwine* contains! It's something like *intermingle* but denser, more secure, and purposeful. Then there's the phrase *overwhelmed with bliss*. Stop for a moment and allow it to paint a picture in your mind. According to this verse, you'll see more of his promises, mercy, love, and grace flow into your life as you entwine your heart in him. Indeed, it says you'll be overwhelmed with bliss. How could this possibly be true?

Do you dare form hope around this promise?

Is "Pray and Read Your Bible" Enough?

The standard answer to "How do I go deeper with God?" is "Pray and read your Bible." But that didn't work for me. I didn't know what to pray, and the words of the Bible felt flat and lifeless. God always seemed far away. The Bible says, "Draw near to God, and he will draw near to you" (James 4:8). Great. So, what could I do since I didn't know how to "draw near" and no one could tell me?

Then, I Saw It!

One verse of Scripture reveals the simple truth about drawing near to God.

For to be carnally <u>minded</u> is death, but to be
spiritually minded *is <u>life and peace</u>. (Romans 8:6)*

God's the only source of true life and peace. Your life's dominant mindset determines whether life and peace manifest in you through your relationship with him.

Your Daily Prime Time

My friend, my heart's greatest desire is to guide you toward a closer, more intimate relationship with God. I'll share key understandings that can change your mindset. I'll offer my devotional routine for coming deep into God's heart. I want your quiet time with God to go from a daily habit to the prime time of your life.

*... **Overwhelmed with bliss** are <u>all</u> who will **<u>entwine</u>
<u>their hearts in him</u>**, waiting for him to help them.
(Isaiah 30:18b TPT)*

Yes, indeed! Wrap great hope around this amazing promise. It is possible to live in heavenly bliss, fulfilled and satisfied in every circumstance. Are you ready?

CHAPTER ONE

CREATED FOR INTIMACY?

Pure love demands an object. Love has no purpose unless it's returned by the one loved.

> *Beloved, let us love one another, **for love is of God**; and everyone who loves is born of God and knows God. He who does not love does not know God, **for God is love**. (1 John 4:7-8)*

Most of us believe that God is love, but we can't express what that means. When we try, we're faced with memories of human love. We only know flawed human love that can comfort and soothe one minute and lash out in frustration or anger the next. Human love can engender trust and devotion and then betray that trust.

God's love isn't that way. Think of it like this: Suppose you encounter a mass of pure, undiluted, living love. What do you think it would say to you? What would it want more than anything? I believe pure love can only say, "I love *you*." And I think it would only want *you* to love it back.

God's love is nothing but a vapor unless there's an object to receive it. It can't be fulfilled unless its object *willingly* loves in return. If you've experienced unrequited love, you know what I'm talking about. God didn't create the universe and everything in it just to show himself how amazing he is.

He created it all for the object of his love, *you.*
He longs for *you* to love him back.

Humans Were Created for Relationship

*Then God said, "Let Us make **man in Our image**, according to **Our likeness;** let them have **dominion** over the fish of the sea, over the birds of the air, and over the cattle, over all the earth and over every creeping thing that creeps on the earth."*
(Genesis 1:26)

This scripture lists the three essential characteristics of a suitable object of God's love. He created humanity with all three of them.

First, humans were created in God's *image* (resemblance). They were the same kind of beings as God. John 4:24 says God is Spirit. So, humans were created as spiritual beings.

Second, they were created according to God's *likeness* (nature or character). They had his holiness, preferences, ways, characteristics, and attitudes.

Finally, God granted humans *dominion* (rule or reign) over the earth and everything in it. They didn't need God's permission about anything in their lives. They reigned supreme on the earth. They had free will to choose and decide independently from God.

> *And the LORD God formed man of the dust of the ground, and **breathed into his nostrils the breath of life**; and man became **a living being**. (Genesis 2:7)*

The first human, Adam, came alive with the life of God himself. He was sinless and free to choose the course of his life. He was the perfect candidate for the deep love relationship God hoped for. God created Eve to be a companion for Adam and gave them only one rule.

> *"... but of the **tree of the knowledge of good and evil you shall not eat**, for in the day that **you eat of it <u>you</u> shall surely die**." (Genesis 2:17)*

And they blew it. The enemy showed up with his lust for power and deceived them by proclaiming that the knowledge of good and evil would make them like God. They believed the lie, ate the forbidden fruit, and their spirits died. They became utterly self-focused, tainting humanity with a sinful nature.

Redeemed for Relationship

The only outcome for sinful mankind was to die physically and spend eternity without any spiritual connection to life. There could be no interactive love relationship with God unless he came up with a way for humans to regain a sinless nature.

Thankfully, he already had a plan.

For the wages of sin is <u>death</u>, but the gift of God is <u>eternal life</u> through Jesus Christ our Lord.
(Romans 6:23 MEV)

No human could qualify to pay the death penalty for man's sin. So God did it himself.

*And the **Word became flesh** and dwelt among us, and **we beheld His glory**, the glory as of the only begotten of the Father, **full of grace and truth**. (John 1:14)*

*And **He Himself** is the **<u>propitiation [atoning sacrifice, payment in full]</u>** for **our sins**, and <u>not for ours only</u> but **also for the whole world**. (1 John 2:2; square brackets note clarifying or defining information here and all verses following)*

Now, only one thing qualifies a person for a close relationship with God. They must receive Jesus' death for sin as their own by faith. What kind of god would do such an amazing thing? Only the God of love could. And he did.

More than a Ticket to Heaven

I've said all of that to say this: Jesus didn't pay the price for your sin so that you could get a ticket to heaven when you die. Yes, your ticket is ready and confirmed. But you received far more than that when you put your faith in him.

*For God so loved the world that He gave His only begotten Son, that <u>whoever believes in Him</u> **should not perish** but **have <u>everlasting life</u>.** (John 3:16)*

The phrase *should not perish* is your punched ticket to heaven. Jesus said *everlasting life* is his gift for those who believe in him. The word translated as *everlasting* is used later when Jesus defines *eternal* life in his prayer for the disciples.

*And this is **eternal [everlasting] life, that they may <u>know You</u>,** the only true God, and Jesus Christ whom You have sent. (John 17:3)*

God's purpose for redemption is so you may *know* him and Jesus Christ. According to *Strong's Concordance* on *www.biblehub.com*, the word translated as *know* here means to *know and understand*, to *know absolutely*.[1] How can you know anyone absolutely?

I didn't know my mother absolutely, but we finished each other's sentences and continued months-old conversations in the middle of a thought. That's the *knowing* God wants you to have of him. Many Christians want to learn correct doctrine and how the Christian life works. That's a great place to start. Yet, I believe he also wants us to know his heart, deep desires, and the depth of his love for us. He wants us to know what he's thinking and finish his sentences.

The same Greek word for *know* appears in Mary's response to Gabriel's invitation for her to become the mother of Jesus.

*Then Mary said to the angel, "How can this be, **since I do not <u>know</u> a man**?" (Luke 1:34)*

I hope I don't have to explain what she's talking about here—but it's how babies are made. When you make the analogy to a relationship with God, it speaks of a creative unity, a oneness of purpose, and an unspeakable, vulnerable trust *toward each other*. This is the *knowing* God longs for you to have with him.

Qualified for Intimacy with God

I can hear the wheels turning in your head. You're right. It's humanly impossible to be righteous enough, holy enough to have an intimate relationship with God. So God took care of that issue, too—in Jesus.

*... we implore you on Christ's behalf, **be <u>reconciled</u> to God**. For He made Him who knew no sin **to be sin <u>for</u> us**, that <u>we might become</u> the **righteousness of God** in Him. (2 Corinthians 5:20b-21)*

You received *God's* righteousness when you made Jesus your Lord. The Spirit of Christ is the Holy Spirit of God. The righteousness, the holiness, and the purity of God dwell in you because the Spirit of Christ dwells in you. If you're born again, you won't ever be more righteous than you are now. You *are* in right standing with God. And even more.

*But he who is **joined to the Lord [born again]** is <u>**one spirit**</u> **with Him**. (1 Corinthians 6:17)*

Put that scripture on and wear it for a while. At the new birth, your spirit wasn't cleaned up or overhauled. The Spirit of the Lord replaced it. Your new spirit is identical to Jesus' Spirit. God's not looking at your behavior or your attitude. He sees Jesus' Spirit in you and rejoices. You no longer need to wait or worry about whether you're good enough to have a relationship with God. You are in Jesus!

The true goal of salvation is for you to share the intimate love of God with him. He wants you to be in a creative union, one in purpose, and share a vulnerable trust with him throughout eternity—starting now. The God of love waits in your heart with open arms and longs for you to entwine your heart in him.

CHAPTER TWO

WHY PURSUE INTIMACY?

The idea of intimacy with God can seem daunting. "Ok, Sharon," you might say. "God wants me to have a close relationship with him. But what's in it for me? Why should I make the effort?"

You may want to take a deep breath on this one. It could change your life.

God wants an intimate relationship with you because his grace flows into your life through the *quality* of your relationship with him. The flow of God's grace is hindered and restricted by an infrequent or distant relationship. It flows more freely when the relationship is frequently nurtured and more intimate.

Let me show you how this works in Scripture.

Grace Flows Through Deep Knowledge of Him

*__Grace and peace__ be multiplied to **you in the
__knowledge__ of God** and of Jesus our Lord, as His
divine power **has given to us __all things__ that pertain to
life and godliness, through the __knowledge__ of Him**
who called us by glory and virtue (2 Peter 1:2-3)*

The word *knowledge* appears twice in this passage. Both
are translated from the same word, meaning *precise and
correct knowledge, full discernment,* and *first-hand
knowledge.* Remember, God dwells in you in the Spirit of
Christ. So, everything you need for life and godliness, grace,
and peace also dwell in you. They are released into your life
as you have first-hand, fully discerned knowledge of God and
his promises.

However, you don't get that kind of knowledge from
hearing a flawed human talk about it. Nor from reading the
words in the Bible only with your limited mental abilities.
John 6:63 says *the Word of God is spirit and life.* Knowledge
of God and his promises is spiritually revealed as you read the
Word through your relationship with him.

The Flow of Protection and Honor

God's heart wants to protect and deliver you from the
enemy's plan to kill, steal, and destroy your life. Life is hard.
There are always challenges to face. God wants to do far more
for you in them than hold your hand and comfort your sorrow.
He wants to deliver and protect you. Please take a few minutes

and read Psalm 91. I invite you to make a list of the promises he makes. You'll be astonished.

Most Christians wish these promises were manifest in their lives but rarely see victory. The problem is the required *conditions* that release the flow of God's protection and deliverance aren't being met. The conditions are laid out in verses 1, 9, and 14.

*He who **dwells** in **the secret place of the Most High***
Shall abide under the shadow of the Almighty.
(Psalm 91:1)

The word *dwell* means to *sit, abide, remain,* and *inhabit.* It's where you live your life and make your home. The first condition is to inhabit and remain in the Most High's secret place. The secret place is in the Spirit of God within you. It's up to you to go there or not. God doesn't come and engulf you and drag you into the secret place. To meet the requirement of verse 1, choose to make the Spirit of God your primary dwelling place.

Verse 9 underscores this understanding and adds another revelation about your dwelling place. It's a refuge.

*Because you have made the LORD, who is my **refuge**,*
*Even **the Most High, your dwelling place**,*
(Psalm 91:9)

The word translated as *refuge* means a *shelter you run into.* It refers to a *shelter from danger and falsehood.* His shelter reveals lies and keeps you safe. Notice that you need to be *in* the shelter for it to protect you. The shelter doesn't come hopping after you while you fight the danger. It stands ready, as close as your breath. Enter instantly by faith. It's your secret dwelling place, your relationship with God.

There's one more conditional scripture, verse 14. It's my favorite. God is the speaker.

> *Because **he has <u>set his love</u> upon Me**, <u>therefore</u> I will deliver him; I will set him on high, because **he has <u>known My name</u>**. (Psalm 91:14)*

You invest your heart and your deepest affection in someone when you choose to *set* your love on them. God will reveal himself to you in ways you can't imagine when you fix your love on him. You will come to know him as he truly is, and he will respond to your love. Here's what God says he will do.

> *He shall <u>call upon Me</u>, and I will <u>answer him</u>; I will <u>be with him in trouble</u>; I will <u>deliver him</u> and <u>honor him</u>. **With <u>long life</u> I will <u>satisfy</u> him, And <u>show him My salvation</u>**. (Psalm 91:15-16)*

I don't know about you, but I'm not satisfied yet. There's more praise to give him, more love to share. And he shows me his salvation every moment of my life.

When you set your love on God, you open the door to your secret place in him. It's the place where his love and grace abound. Protection, deliverance, honor, and long life are yours as you dwell in a close relationship with God.

The Flow of Wisdom and Guidance

We live in a world that is noisy and complex. If we need anything from God, wisdom and guidance top the list. They are both readily available from within the intimacy of your relationship with him. Let's look at Proverbs 3:5-8, starting with verse 5.

> **Trust in the Lord _completely_**, and do not rely on your own opinions. **_With all your heart_ rely on him to guide you**, and he **will lead you in every decision you make**. (Proverbs 3:5 TPT)

How do you trust God completely? Start by admitting you aren't as smart as you think you are. God is infinitely wiser than you and sees beyond the present into what lies ahead. Doubt and unbelief deafen you to God's voice and open the door to the enemy. Cast doubt far away and trust God. That trust is the foundation of a close relationship with him.

> **Become _intimate_ with him** in _whatever you do_, and he **will lead you** _wherever you go_. (Proverbs 3:6 TPT)

There it is in a nutshell. Intimacy with God welcomes his guidance in everything.

> Don't think for a moment that you know it all, **for _wisdom comes_ when you _adore_ him with _undivided devotion_** and avoid everything that's wrong. (Proverbs 3:7 TPT)

Wisdom comes when your devotion to God is undivided. Check yourself. Who are you more devoted to than him? Look, love isn't a zero-sum commodity. All your other relationships are enhanced, not weakened when God is your intimate partner in life. Wisdom comes when intimacy with God is paramount.

> ***Then*** *you will find the* ***healing refreshment*** *your body and spirit long for. (Proverbs 3:8 TPT)*

My dear friend, your whole being is refreshed by your devotion to the Lord. Wisdom, guidance, and healing come supernaturally as you nurture an intimate love relationship with him.

God Eagerly Flows Grace Through Intimacy with Him

Let's look again at Isaiah 30:18. The previous verses reveal Israel's rebellion and self-reliance. They also show God's hope that they would return to him and be forgiven and restored to favor.

> *For this reason the* **Lord is still** <u>*waiting*</u> *to show his favor to you so he can* **show you his marvelous love.** **He** <u>**waits**</u> **to be gracious to you.** *He sits on his throne [*"he will be exalted" in the NKJV]* **ready to show mercy to you.** *For YAHWEH is the Lord of justice,* **faithful to keep his promises.** <u>**Overwhelmed with bliss**</u>

*are all who will <u>entwine</u> their hearts in him, waiting
for him to help them. (Isaiah 30:18 TPT)*

No matter what Israel's rebellious history was, God was
ready to flood Israel with grace, love, and mercy if they would
return and entwine their hearts in him. He feels the same way
about you. Nothing in your life can hinder God's love for you.
He waits for you to pursue intimacy with him and responds
with the flow of grace.

God is eager to release his grace into your life. Yes, he
waits for you to enter his presence. But he isn't dozing on the
throne or playing solitaire while he waits. Both *waits* and
waiting are translated from the same Hebrew word meaning
longing or *waiting in ambush.*

I pondered *waiting in ambush* when I first studied this
verse. As I did, God played a video for the eyes of my heart.

A grandmother waited for her grandkids to come and
spend the day with her. She had treats and gifts ready for each
of them, sorted by name. She looked at her watch. "Oh,
they're almost here!" She ran to the living room window and
peered down the road. Nothing. She ran to the front door and
looked through the side light. Still nothing. Then, back to the
window. "Here they come!" Back to the front door. "They're
here!"

As they reached for the screen, she jerked open the front
door. She grabbed the first one, twirled him around with joy,
and smothered him with wet grandma kisses. Wiping his
moisture-covered face with his sleeve, he headed for the plate
of cookies on the counter. She pulled the next one close,

hugging her so tight their heartbeats synchronized. Tears of joy flowed freely.

That's the way God is about you. He longs for you to engage him in a close love relationship. He wants you to know his heart the way he knows yours. He wants to flow his grace into your life through your relationship with him.

Here's how the scripture would read if there were a "Sharon" translation:

> God _eagerly waits to ambush you with His grace_ when you come to enjoy His company. He rises for you and _keeps every promise._ _He floods you with mercy and meets every need._ You eagerly anticipate every moment with Him. _The bliss of His grace overwhelms you_ as you **entwine your heart in him in an ever-deepening love relationship.**

God's always working to get his goodness into your life. He can work through the limited prayers of others but prefers the direct route of a love relationship with you. The closer and more intimate it is, the easier his love and grace flow.

Choose to entwine your heart in him today.

CHAPTER THREE

WHAT'S HOLDING YOU BACK

Y ou're reading this book because you want a deeper relationship with God. Maybe you feel hesitant or worried about how God will respond. If so, you likely have an incomplete or incorrect understanding of the true nature of God. No one knows God perfectly. However, pursuing a closer relationship with him is nearly impossible if you believe in false traditions about crucial aspects of his nature.

The place to start is submitted to the truth. Put aside your automatic expectations, preconceived notions, and judgments over past experiences. Develop an "I know nothing; show me, Lord" attitude.

*Beware lest anyone **cheat you through philosophy and <u>empty deceit</u>, <u>according to the tradition of men</u>,** according to the <u>basic principles of the world</u>, **and not according to <u>Christ</u>**. (Colossians 2:8)*

Most incorrect doctrines aren't malicious. They come from good-hearted people sharing what they've learned from their teachers or the church quarterly. They're taught by tradition, not by revelation of God's Word. Be quick to discard false doctrine when you see the truth. You cheat yourself of God's grace when you cling to a doctrine that opposes the Word of God.

Lies of the Enemy Hold You Back

Satan doesn't care if you believe in God. He certainly doesn't like that you're born again. But he hates watching you worship and obey God. He wants to deceive you about God's mercy and goodness.

The enemy accomplishes his objective either by:

- Convincing you God is angry or disappointed for the sin in your life.
- Or convincing you to blame God for something horrible that Satan did.

Let's deal with these two powerful lies. Knowing the truth will set you free from them.

Lie #1: You Failed God, and He's Mad at You

There are four common expressions of this lie in the church today. You may recognize one if you think God is mad or wants to punish you. Remember, these are *lies* of the enemy.

Resulting Wrong Beliefs

Because of your sin or failure:

- You lose your salvation. You must repent, confess, and be born again, again.
- You risk losing your salvation. You must repent, confess, and be forgiven before you die.
- You don't lose your salvation, but God withholds blessings and won't talk to you. You must repent, confess, and be forgiven before he considers you worthy of attention.
- You don't lose your salvation, but God punishes you with something evil. He'll put sickness, calamity, or poverty on you to teach you something.

Every one of these doctrines is false. The verses used to back them don't consider the whole counsel of the Word. Jesus' atonement paid for forgiveness, healing, peace, and prosperity in every aspect of life. God won't use anything Jesus defeated on the cross against you.

Be Completely Reconciled to God

It's time to receive complete freedom from the bondage of sin. Put away sin's guilt, condemnation, and remorse. Be reconciled to God.

> *that is, that* **God was in Christ** *reconciling the world to Himself,* **not counting their sins against them***, and has entrusted to us the message of reconciliation. ...* **We implore you** *in Christ's stead:* **Be reconciled to God***. (2 Corinthians 5:19,20b MEV)*

The word translated as *world* in this verse means the *cosmos of existence and all its inhabitants*. That includes every human who has ever lived on the Earth or ever will, including you. God isn't counting your sinful behavior against you. His scale of justice only measures whether you put your faith in the finished work of Jesus.

My dear Christian friend, receive this word of reconciliation. God came to earth in Jesus. He took all your sin into himself and paid the debt of death you owed. He erased your indictment of sin with the blood of Christ. He's not counting any sin against you, past, present, or future. You are forgiven. Walk free.

Walk in the Righteousness of God

Go ahead. Walk free of guilt and shame. Walk in the freedom of his righteousness.

> *For He made **Him who knew no sin to be sin for us**, that we might **become the righteousness of God** in **Him**. (2 Corinthians 5:21)*

Receive this truth. God is never mad or disappointed with you. He never punishes you for sin. He already punished Jesus for it. You are now as righteous as God is! How could he be upset with you?

One point of clarification is needed. The freedom *from* sin in Christ isn't freedom *to* sin. Yes, all your sins are forgiven, but any sin still has negative consequences. It doesn't change God's love for you but draws you away from him and hardens your heart toward him. Moreover, it opens the door for Satan to try to destroy your life, your family, and your purpose.

Instead of hiding from God when you sin, run to his arms. Repent. Thank him joyfully for forgiving you. Receive his love. Then get up, dust yourself off, and do better.

Lie #2: God Seemed to Fail You, and You're Mad at Him

Sometimes, people take offense at God because of a difference between what they expect to happen and reality. Maybe they prayed for a healing that didn't happen. Perhaps they were hurt by the church or a Christian who got away with it. Maybe their life was ruined by a calamity. Satan is the one to blame for those things, not God.

Put the Blame Where it Belongs

Life is hard for everybody. But there's never a reason to blame God. When Adam and Eve believed Satan's lies, the devil got his hands on the world. The enemy has run roughshod over humanity ever since. You can have peace in every situation because of the victory of Jesus' finished work.

> *"I have told you these things so that **in Me you may have peace**. In the world you will have tribulation. But be of good cheer. **I have overcome the world**."*
> *(John 16:33 MEV)*

The Word says God is faithful and keeps his promises (Hebrews 10:23). If your prayers aren't working as expected, *you're* missing something. It's a reason to get closer to God and study the Word, not to blame him.

> *The _thief_ does not come, except to **steal and kill and destroy**. I came that they **may have** _life_, and that they **may have it** _more abundantly_. (John 10:10)*

And,

> *Do not be _deceived_, my beloved brethren. **Every _good_ _gift_ and every _perfect gift_ is from _above_, and comes down _from the Father_ of lights**, with whom _there is no variation or shadow of turning_. (James 1:16-17)*

God doesn't put tragedy in your life. If it's something intended to steal "good" from you, steer you toward death, or destroy you, it's the devil's doing. If it leads you toward abundant life, it's God's blessing.

If it's good, it's from God. If it's bad, it's from the devil. It's that simple.

Engage the New Covenant and Embrace the God of Grace

You were raised with rules. They're essential for society to function in peace. However, the Mosaic Law, the Old Covenant, was established to show the Hebrew people it was impossible to be good enough to please God. It was intended to show them they needed a savior.

They had to obey *every* law to qualify for the blessings of God. Broken laws and sin required a death payment. Rather than kill the sinner, God put animal sacrifices in place. The sins of the people were symbolically placed on an animal, which was then killed. Thus, a substitute paid the penalty, and the sinner lived.

But that covenant solved nothing. It only pointed the way to the covenant God wanted. His heart longed for a people who could love him and on whom he could lavish grace. Here's how he explained it through Jeremiah:

> "No, this is the **new covenant** I will make with the people of Israel when the time has come," declares YAHWEH. "I will <u>embed my law into the core of their being and write it on their hearts and minds</u>. **Then I will truly be their God**, and they will **truly be my people**. None of them will have to teach their friends or family, saying, 'Come and know YAHWEH intimately!' No, from the least to the greatest, **they will all <u>know me intimately</u>**," YAHWEH declares, "for I will **<u>remove their guilt and wipe their sin from my memory</u>**." (Jeremiah 31:33-34 TPT)

God longed for a people who would *know him intimately*. Their sin would no longer hinder their relationship with him. Under this new covenant, God would *remove their guilt and wipe their sin from his memory*.

My dear friend, that's the covenant Jesus secured. Jesus wasn't a temporary substitute sacrifice for your sin. God put all sin of all people for all time on sinless Jesus. He paid the penalty and died. But, unlike animal sacrifices, he rose again to life, victorious over death, hell, and the grave. All you did to receive his payment as yours was put your faith in his selfless act. Through Jesus, God removed your guilt and wiped all your sins from his memory.

You qualify for an intimate relationship with God. He's waiting for you like an eager grandma with a pile of gifts that bear your name. Will you come?

CHAPTER FOUR

SPIRIT TO SPIRIT

Human relationships involve your mind and body. You go places, do things, and talk with human friends in the natural, physical realm. God is Spirit. So, how can you develop a relationship with God, who's in the spiritual realm? It's simpler than you might think.

> You get to know God in his environment,
> spirit (us) to Spirit (him).

It's easy to have a valuable but shallow relationship with God: You get born again, go to church now and then, live any way you want, pray when things get tough, then die and go to heaven. Indeed, being with God in heaven is the greatest gift you can receive. But there's so much more he wants to do for you now, in this life, through your relationship with him. All that's required to get started is to meet him regularly, spirit to Spirit.

In the Spirit

Jesus revealed God's desire for a close relationship with his children to the Samaritan woman at the well.

*"But the hour is coming, and **now is**, when the **true worshipers** will worship the Father in spirit and truth; for the **Father is seeking such to worship Him**. **God is Spirit**, and those who worship Him **must** worship in **spirit and truth** [reality, sincerity]."*
(John 4:23-24)

In today's world, *worship* can be a remote thing. People voice their gratefulness and appreciation at church and think little about it the rest of the week. They may have a genuine experience with God, but it's often over before the offering is received.

The word translated as *worshiper* in this verse means *one who adores*. The online version of the *Oxford English Dictionary* defines *adore* as *loving and respecting someone deeply*.[2] Jesus said we **must [love and respect God deeply] in spirit** and truth.

If you want a deep relationship with God, you must *meet with him in the spirit realm* where he resides. He waits there for *you* to come to him.

"Okay," you might say. "But meeting God in the spirit realm is impossible. I'm stuck here in the flesh and have no clue how to get God's attention, much less meet him in the throne room." I hear you. I used to say the same thing. For years, God remained a distant, distracted deity while I faced my challenges alone. That is until I learned about basic Christian anatomy.

Your Christian Anatomy

You function most effectively as a Christian when you know the parts of your Christian anatomy and how they relate to each other. Paul, the writer of 1 Thessalonians, understood humans to be comprised of three distinct parts: a spirit, a soul, and a body.

Now may the God of peace Himself sanctify you **completely;** *and may your* **whole spirit, soul, and body** *be preserved blameless at the coming of our Lord Jesus Christ. (1 Thessalonians 5:23)*

The Body

The Greek word translated as *body* in this verse is *soma* and refers to the *physical body of a human or animal.* Your body is your physical earth suit. It carries your life's essence around from place to place, enabling you to interact with your earthly environment. It has sensory interfaces that relay sight, sound, smell, taste, and touch indicators to your brain. The brain interprets the indicators and directs the body accordingly. Your body is what other people perceive when they encounter you.

The Soul

The word translated as *soul* here refers to a *person's distinct identity.* It is the *seat of the mind, will, emotions, and personality*. It's part of your life's essence. It helps interpret input from your five senses and can trigger your body to respond in specific ways. It's not physical and can't be perceived by physical means. However, other people's souls easily experience yours. It's powerful beyond your awareness. It can bless people and nurture them. Or it can curse them and hurt them deeply.

The Spirit

Your spirit is undetectable by anyone's five senses or soul. You only know you have a spirit because you're alive.

> *For as the **body without the spirit** is **dead**, so faith without works is dead also. (James 2:26)*

Your spirit doesn't cause any physical sensations. But you may experience a physical response to worship triggered by your soul. It may cause goosebumps, tears, or other emotional reactions when it encounters a fruit of the Spirit, such as God's love, joy, or peace.

The Heart

The Greek word most often translated as *heart* in the New Testament is *kardia*. It means *the sense of physical life* and *the seat of intelligence, will, and character*. Your heart is the combination of your non-physical parts, your spirit and soul.

The Flesh

> *Jesus answered, "Most assuredly, I say to you, unless
> one is born of water and the Spirit, he cannot enter the
> kingdom of God. **That which is born of the flesh is
> <u>flesh</u>, and that which is born of the Spirit is <u>spirit</u>.***
> *(John 3:5-6)*

The word translated as *flesh* in this passage means the *physical body* or *human nature and desires, including the soul*. Here, Jesus revealed the most basic understanding of the word *flesh*. It's the part of you that isn't your spirit. Your flesh is the combination of your body and soul.

Christians often use the word *flesh* with an evil or sinful connotation. But that understanding is too narrow. Yes, all sin is fleshly, but not all fleshy things are sinful. Quilting is a fleshly hobby that involves a creative mind and the body's sewing skills. But quilting isn't generally seen as a sinful hobby.

The Christian System

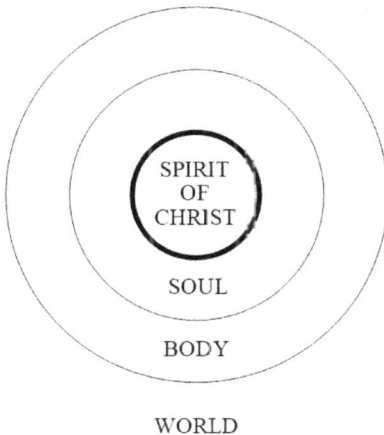

WORLD

Here's a picture of what I've been talking about. Remember, the Spirit of Christ dwells in every born-again believer.

Your body is your physical part, interfacing with the world and reporting its findings to the soul. Your soul processes the findings and tells the body how to respond. Here's the part few Christians realize: *Your soul can interface with your spirit!* You encountered this if you ever experienced God's love, mercy, or peace during worship.

This was the missing key for my relationship with God. I *know* God's mercy. Several years ago, I had to make a tough decision and worried I'd make the wrong one. But the mercy of God gently engulfed me with tangible assurance of his love and forgiveness no matter what my decision was. Yes, my soul knows the mercy of the Spirit of God quite well.

Make the Soul-Spirit Connection

It is simple to connect your awareness to the Spirit of God. Just *turn your attention* to spiritual things.

I learned this truth while watching an online Bible college class called *Walking in the Spirit*. I stood up out of my chair. "Why wasn't I taught this by my Spirit-filled pastor thirty-five years ago," I asked myself. "Was he blind to it, too?" I hope you get the revelation here. It is so simple to *move into the Spirit* that you might want to shout. Well, go ahead.

*For those who **live according to the flesh <u>set their minds</u>** on the things of the flesh, but those who **live according to the Spirit, [<u>set their minds</u> on]** the things of the Spirit. For to be carnally [fleshly] minded is death, but to be <u>**spiritually minded is life and peace**</u>.*
(Romans 8:5-6)

Most people let their minds drift from one thing to the next unless they're worried. Then they set their minds on that worrisome thing and stew about it all day. Learn to control your thoughts (2 Corinthians 10:5). You can choose to *set your mind on the things of the Spirit*. When you do, you'll instantly be in the flow of God's life and peace.

I invite you to practice choosing to think about spiritual things. You may feel a bit awkward at first, but keep trying. God will welcome you with Spirit hugs. Here are some things you could think about:

- Consider the scripture shown above (Romans 8:5-6)
- Your salvation and God's forgiveness
- Something wonderful God did for you and how grateful you are
- Jesus at God's right hand
- What the River of Life looks like
- Something amazing you read in the Word

When your thoughts drift to fleshly things, bring them back to focus on spiritual things. See how easy that is?

Welcome to the Presence of God.

CHAPTER FIVE

IMAGINATION:
YOUR SPIRITUAL EYES

E very thought that enters your head arrives on the screen of your imagination. Every memory or hunch emerges into your awareness on the same screen. Even the aha moment of divine revelation comes to life in the part of you that sees what isn't visible and hears what isn't audible. Your imagination is the seat of creativity and the scratchpad of your reasoning process. It's God's divine threshold between your soul and his spiritual realm.

You may be a little nervous about using your imagination for spiritual reasons. Maybe you've been warned about accessing the wrong realm through guided imagery. I agree. Caution is warranted, especially if the guide's spiritual intent is unknown. But what if God is guiding you?

Consider how God keeps you in perfect peace.

*You [God] will keep him in **perfect peace**, Whose*
*__mind__ is __stayed__ **on You**, Because he <u>trusts</u> in You.*
(Isaiah 26:3)

In this verse, *mind* is translated from a Hebrew word
meaning *imagination, conception,* or *what is framed in the
mind.* The Passion Translation nails it.

Perfect, absolute peace *surrounds those whose*
__imaginations are consumed__ *with you; they*
confidently <u>trust</u> *in you. (Isaiah 26:3 TPT)*

Perfect, absolute peace is the pure fruit of the Holy Spirit.
It doesn't come from any other source. You can't connect
your soul to the wrong spiritual realm when you focus on
God's spiritual things. He designed your imagination to usher
you into his presence.

Jesus Used His Holy Imagination

Jesus was as limited by his physical body as you are. He
couldn't take his body into the heavenly realm and consult
with God about the day's activities. He consulted with God
by prayer and received insight from God by revelation of the
answers, the same way you do.

Then Jesus answered and said to them, "Most assured-
*ly, I say to you, **the Son can do nothing of Himself,***
*but **what He <u>sees</u> the Father do**; for whatever He*
does, the Son also does in like manner. (John 5:19)

What do you think the word *sees* in this scripture means? Jesus didn't see the Spirit of God with his physical eyes. The Greek word translated as *sees* means to *discern mentally, observe,* or *perceive.* Jesus perceived what he saw in the spiritual realm on the screen of his mind's imagination.

"Set Your Mind" is a Mindset Shift

You can't develop a close relationship with anyone with a glance or a brief hello. It takes frequent, uninterrupted time to engage in two-way conversation. Your mental attention must be set and remain focused on the other person for longer than a few seconds.

Look again at Isaiah 26:3.

*You will **keep** him in <u>perfect peace</u>, Whose **mind is stayed** on **You**, Because he trusts in You. (Isaiah 26:3)*

God wants you to have perfect peace all the time. But that's only possible if your mind remains focused on him. The Hebrew word translated as *stayed* means *rests, leans, steadfast,* or *sustained.* You rest your thoughts and attention on God using your imagination. When you do, God can flow his perfect peace into your life.

"How can I keep my mind set on God?" you might ask. "Am I supposed to forget my regular life and be a monk or something?"

Well, can you worry about your problems and still do the dishes? Can you stew about needing money and still do your job? When you worry, you use your imagination to meditate on negative things. Your mind stays focused on the possibility of a terrible outcome. But you still get the job done and take care of the family. You *can* meditate on the things of God and fulfill your life's obligations at the same time. The difference is that you'll do it in peace and joy instead of fear and anxiety.

My friend, choose the new mindset. You've seen how simple it is to set your mind on spiritual things. It's worth learning how to keep it there.

Your Soul is Your Spiritual Valve

Your soul functions as a spiritual valve. It controls God's access to your life through the threshold of your thoughts and imagination. Look again at Romans 8:5-6.

*For those **who live according to the flesh set their minds on the things of the flesh**, but those **who live according to the Spirit, the things of the Spirit**. For <u>to be carnally minded is death</u>, but <u>to be spiritually minded is life and peace</u>. (Romans 8:5-6)*

The words *flesh* and *carnal* in this passage are translated from the same Greek word. They mean the same thing discussed in the previous chapter: your body and soul.

Carnally Minded

To be carnally minded isn't necessarily a wrong or sinful thing. It means the person's thoughts and mental images are dominated by the situations and events of their physical life. But there's a problem with being carnally minded.

*Because the **carnal mind is <u>enmity</u> against God**; for it is not subject to the law of God, nor indeed can be.*
(Romans 8:7)

I know this is hard to hear. But they aren't my words. They are God's truth. You put out the welcome mat to the enemy when your dominant thoughts are on carnal, natural things. You give him access to plant unbelief, anxiety, and other expressions of death into your heart. Worse, you shut down the flow of God's involvement in your life.

Thankfully, God remains faithful. He always wants to flood your life with peace and grace. He'll squeeze out as much love and grace to you as possible with the focus you give him. But he wants to flood your life with grace.

Spiritually Minded

You open the floodgates of life and peace when you *keep* your mind focused on God and his spiritual realm. What's more, you shut down the flow of the enemy's involvement in your life. There may still be challenges to face. But God's guidance, provision, and power will automatically flow to lead you through them toward victory.

When you stay spiritually minded, something miraculous happens. Healing and deliverance flow along with wisdom and joy.

As a kid, my daddy called me a worrywart. I was insecure and worried about everything. It made me suspicious and resentful. Even as an adult, my mind was set on the cares of this life, and I dealt with negative thoughts and situations constantly.

A few years ago, God activated his call on my life, and I enrolled in Bible college. After only four months of intense study in the Word and spending more time with the Lord in prayer, my husband said, "You're a lot nicer than you used to be." Yes, I knew. Joy filled my heart. I was calmer and more peaceful. And I loved my husband more sweetly than ever. All without trying. Revelations of God's Word and the wonders of his love for me dominated my thoughts and imagination. Spiritual-mindedness opened the flow of healing, grace, and peace into my life, transforming me.

The devil still tries to get on my case when I'm tired. But I catch on quickly and redirect my thoughts to the Lord.

How to Become More Spiritually Minded

The minds and imaginations of most Christians are dominated by the cares and events of their natural lives. It's basic human nature and the only option unsaved people have. But you have a choice. God's grace-realities can dominate your thoughts if you make the effort.

Discover the True Nature of God and What He Did for You in Jesus

How can you meditate on God's nature and how he relates to you by grace if you don't know what he said about those things in the New Testament? Study the Word straight from the Word. Use messages and books by great teachers. Check out what they say by studying the scriptures they use for yourself.

I recommend the following books by Andrew Wommack: *The True Nature of God; The New You & The Holy Spirit; Spirit, Soul, & Body;* and *The Believer's Authority.*

Control Your Dominant Thoughts

Yes, you can train yourself to think primarily about spiritual things.

> *For the weapons of our warfare are not carnal, but mighty through God to the **pulling down of strongholds**, casting down **imaginations and every high thing** that exalts itself **against the knowledge of God**, bringing every thought into captivity to the obedience of Christ,* (2 Corinthians 10:4-5 MEV)

The battles in your life aren't about the situations and people you deal with. They're about *how you think* about them. The beliefs and thoughts that dominate you are strongholds of the enemy if they are contrary to what God says. Grab that contrary thought when it zings through your head and cast it down. Replace it with the words of grace and truth the Bible says about the situation.

For example, Satan occasionally accuses me of being too inadequate to write. I respond to that thought with a sharp "No." "I rebuke that thought and cast it down. God called me to this work and equips me with everything I need to complete it. Thank you, Lord," I say out loud with zeal. See 1 Timothy 1:12 for the scripture that backs me up.

Remove Worldly-Minded Input from Your Life

It's hard to stay spiritually minded when you invite ungodly and evil things into your heart. What you read, the music you listen to, and the television programs and movies you watch *matter*. It's time to make better choices if you want your dominant thoughts to be more godly.

> *And now, dear brothers and sisters, one final thing.*
> **Fix your thoughts** *on what is* **true, and honorable, and right, and pure, and lovely, and admirable.** *Think about things that are* **excellent and worthy of praise.**
> **Keep putting into practice** *all you learned and received from me*-everything you heard from me and saw me doing. **Then** *the* **God of peace will be with you.** *(Philippians 4:8-9 NLT)*

I give you unconditional permission to remove ungodly media influences from your life. Sometimes, it's necessary to make relationship changes. I'll leave that permission for you to work out with God.

Here are some ideas to consider:

- Stop watching the news.
- Select more wholesome movies.
- Make more time for prime time with God.
- Listen to good Bible teachers in the car.
- Set boundaries with toxic relationships.
- Read Christian fiction.
- Play worship music at home and in the car.
- Select better television programming.

Oh, my friend. As you reprogram your imagination to meditate on spiritual things, you'll become more aware of God's presence, moment by moment. Gratitude will fill your heart and spill over the edges with joy. And you'll gladly entwine your heart in him.

CHAPTER SIX

THE SECRET PLACE

When you want to have a private conversation with someone, you probably don't meet them in a noisy, busy place. I pulled into the parking lot of the grocery store one day. As I parked in my space, I saw my quilting buddy getting into the car facing me. We quickly greeted each other with a hug, and off we went. It wasn't the time or place to have a deep conversation. We'd get into personal things the next time we sewed together in my studio.

The same is true regarding getting to know God. You get *inspired* at church or Sunday school but can only get to know him personally in private, one-to-one conversations.

God's reserved the perfect place just for you.

Your Secret Place

God has a private place permanently booked in your name. He has secrets to share with you there.

> *There's a **private place** reserved for the **devoted lovers**
> of YAHWEH, where they **sit near him** and **receive the**
> **revelation-secrets** of his promises. (Psalm 25:14 TPT)*

He has personal insights to reveal, much like lovers who openly share their hearts, deepest desires, and cherished secrets. He craves your companionship and your devotion. He's given everything to win your heart. He's made it easy for you to find him—in that private, secret place.

You Are Not Separate from Him

A close, intimate relationship with God isn't a Bible metaphor or empty religious jargon. God's a living spirit who loves you and longs for intimate conversation and fellowship. The only possible way is to get out of your physical and mental limitations and meet him in person in the *spiritual* realm.

You meet God in the spiritual realm every time you enter worship and when he shows you something special in the Scriptures. But do you *abide* there? Do you live your everyday life *while* you fellowship with God? That's the kind of relationship he's looking for. Like a good marriage, he wants you to live your life united in love and purpose with him—joined at the heart. That's only possible with a revelation of being one spirit with him. Remember this scripture from chapter one?

*But he who is **joined to the Lord** is <u>**one spirit**</u> **with Him**. (1 Corinthians 6:17)*

I knew in my head that the Holy Spirit dwelled in me. I could say I was one spirit with the Lord. But I prayed to a god who was far off in the distance. Sometimes, it felt like God was close, but he was always with me to the side or within me separately. It didn't dawn on me that we were one united spirit until God got in my face about it and put me on the path to intimacy with him.

It happened in a class called *Life Foundations*. The instructor taught on the vine and the branches.

<u>**Abide in Me**</u>*, and I in you. As the **branch** <u>**cannot bear fruit of itself**</u>**,** *unless it* <u>**abides**</u> *in the **vine**,* <u>**neither can you**</u>*, unless you **abide in Me**. (John 15:4)*

He said, "Like the vine's nutritious sap flows through the branches, so God's blood flows through your veins." It was like God finally had enough of my thick skull. He whooshed in close, grabbed me by the collar, and said firmly in my face:

"You. Are. Not. Separate. From. Me."

You're not separate from him, either. Your spirit is already one Spirit with Christ. The only thing left is to get your soul to cooperate, and you'll be with God in person, joined at the heart.

Your Mindset is the Door to Your Secret Place in the Lord

There's no need to get God's attention or wait to be invited into your secret place. Your spirit is his Spirit. His attention and his love are in you and fixed on you. Set your soul's mind on him, and you'll be in your secret place. Turn your soul's attention away from yourself and your problems, challenges, and life's routines. Fill your imagination with God and his goodness, and stay there. Abide in him always. Relax in his peace and let him love you.

It's the Secret Place of God's Grace, not His Wrath

I've already covered this point, but it bears repeating. You never need to be reluctant to fellowship with God in your secret place. He's not mad at you or rolling his eyes. He's not disappointed in you for any of your mistakes.

> *For **God did not appoint us to wrath**, but to obtain salvation through our Lord Jesus Christ, **who died for us**, that whether we wake or sleep, we should **live together with Him**. (1Thessalonians 5:9-10)*

God's thrilled to greet you in your secret place. He waits there like a love-struck grandma expecting her grandbaby. He waits there so he can lavish you with grace.

*Let us therefore **come boldly** to the **throne of <u>grace</u>**,
that we may **obtain <u>mercy</u>** and **find <u>grace</u>** to help in
time of need. (Hebrews 4:16)*

Privacy in the Secret Place

Jesus often escaped the press and noise of the crowd when he needed to hear from God.

*Now in the morning, having risen a long while before
daylight, He went out and **departed to a <u>solitary place</u>**;
and **there He <u>prayed</u>**. (Mark 1:35)*

The secret place was so important to Jesus that he taught about it in the Sermon on the Mount.

*But you, when you pray, **go into your room**, and when
you have **<u>shut your door</u>**, pray to your Father **who is
in the <u>secret place</u>**; and your Father <u>who sees in secret</u>
will <u>reward you openly</u>. (Matthew 6:6)*

The context here is that prayer is a private conversation with God, not an opportunity to impress people with how spiritual you are. You're not required to pray in a closet with the door shut. You're welcome in the secret place even if you're in a crowded airport. But God wants a *private* conversation with you. The flow of grace and wisdom is interrupted by every distraction, and he doesn't want you to miss out on a thing.

Your secret place is the intimacy of your relationship with the Lord. He's waiting for you to come. Use your imagination to set your mind on him, then move in closer.

Entwine your heart in him and enjoy the bliss of his love in your secret place.

CHAPTER SEVEN

HEARING GOD

G od's Word is clear. He wants a deep, interactive relationship with you. Hearing what he says to you is the key.

*that which we have seen and heard we declare to you, that **you also may have <u>fellowship</u> with us**; and truly our fellowship is <u>**with the Father**</u> **and** <u>**with His Son Jesus Christ**</u>. (1 John 1:3)*

John shared his love for God from personal experience. It wasn't his theory or what someone else reported. He had true fellowship with the Father and with Christ. The word *fellowship* is translated from Greek, meaning *an intimate bond* or *communion between people with great benefit for both*. The online version of the *Cambridge Dictionary* defines *communion* as a *close relationship in which thoughts and feelings are exchanged*.[3]

Going deeper with God involves learning to communicate with him, both speaking and listening to him. Most people pray by reminding God of all the awful things going on in their lives and presenting him with a laundry list of action items. God cares about both things, but they can't produce fellowship or guidance. God has beautiful plans for your life, but they'll never happen unless you hear and follow his direction.

There are three primary reasons why you may not hear God speak even though he talks to you constantly.

First, you may dominate the conversation; he can't get a word in edgewise. I suggest you ask him questions, pause, and listen for his answers.

Second, your spiritual ears may be clogged up with carnal clamor. The noise of the world may have your head distracted and worried. Stop, shut out the world's input, and reset your imagination and attention onto God's goodness.

And third, you may not know how God speaks to you. It's easier to recognize his voice when you know how he speaks to his children.

You Do Hear His Voice

My sheep hear My voice, and I know them, and they follow Me. (John 10:27)

God has the answer to every need. It's always the best answer for your situation; he wants to share it with you. Other voices in your life may drown out God's right now. But his voice will become familiar when you can finally hear it.

You slap the enemy with a gag order when you worship the Lord. Faith always comes when you hear the Word in your heart. So, when you hear God speak, faith in his words will explode in your heart. You'll know his voice and walk in his guidance by that faith.

Ways God Speaks to His Children

Remember, God is Spirit. He speaks to your spirit in the spiritual secret place of your heart. If you're arguing with someone and you think punching them in the nose is the best option, you didn't hear it from God. Abide in him. Have your heart tuned in to his frequency. That's when you'll hear him.

Here are some ways God speaks to your heart, as found in Scripture.

The Still, Small Voice in Your Heart

> Then He said, "Go out, and stand on the mountain before the LORD." ... and after the earthquake a fire, but **the LORD was not in the fire**; and **after the fire a still small voice**. So it was, **when Elijah heard it [the still, small voice]**, that he wrapped his face in his mantle and went out and stood in the entrance of the cave. (1 Kings 19:11a, 12-13a)

Elijah was in a cave when God told him, in a still, small voice, to stand on the mountain. God performed a mighty demonstration of his power with wind, earthquake, and fire. But his presence and his voice weren't in all that commotion. God's voice was quiet, just a whisper. Elijah didn't hear it over the wind and earthquake. He heard God in his heart, not with his ears.

You use your mind and imagination constantly. Whatever you're thinking about moves logically to the next thought. The ones that follow aren't random; there's a connection to what came before. For example, suppose I think about chicken salad. That triggers a memory of a picnic when I was thirteen. That thought leads to one about the ballroom dance lessons I took at that age, which leads to a popular song. I can't remember the words, so I make up silly lyrics and dissolve into laughter. Suddenly, I'm a world away from chicken salad. But all my thoughts connect.

The thought God gives you in his still, small voice is a *knowing* that doesn't fit your current train of thought. It comes out of the blue, apparently random, but wise. You know in your believing knower that you heard from God.

He used his still, small voice to activate his call on my life. I sat in my recliner minding my business when my brain suddenly received understanding. He asked, "Well, are you coming?" I didn't hear the words with my ears, but I knew the question. I quickly replied, "Where should I start?"

God's whisper is knowing without hearing. You don't think it in sequence with other thoughts. It just shows up in your understanding. That's God's heart speaking to yours.

The Revelation of Life in His Word

Most Christians read the Bible on the surface. The written words on the pages deliver an excellent education in church history and godly behavior. Glory to God for that. Church people taught at this level are good, loving people who care about each other. But God longs for them to know who *he* is, what's in his heart, and his plan for their lives. And he wants to guide them moment by moment through the jungle of the natural world.

God can't speak his heart into yours and court you with his love if you stay on the surface of Bible truth. He wants you to meet him, spirit to Spirit in his Word.

*But as it is written: "Eye has not seen, nor ear heard, Nor have entered into the heart of man **The things which God has prepared** for **those who love Him**." But **God has revealed them** to us **through His Spirit**. For **the Spirit searches** all things, yes, **the deep things of God**. (1 Corinthians 2:9-10)*

My friend, God reveals the deep things he has for you into your *heart's* understanding, not through reading the Bible with your eyes. His words take on a living, breathing component when revealed to you. A depth of understanding opens and invites you to linger with it in your imagination. God can instantly transform you with his revealed word.

God used the revelation of Scripture to confirm my calling as a writer. I knew I was to teach the Word but was overwhelmed with doubt about writing. I was reading 1 Corinthians, chapter 2, during my prime time one day when his life leaped into my heart. He confirmed my calling with this one verse.

> *And we articulate these [grace] realities with the*
> *words imparted to us by the Spirit and not with the*
> *words taught by human wisdom.* **We join together**
> **Spirit-revealed truths with Spirit-revealed words.**
> *(1 Corinthians 2:13 TPT)*

I was transformed into a writer at that moment. All my questions about it were answered. It was settled.

My friend, God has wisdom for your life and the joy of its revelation ready for you in his Word. Approach the Scriptures with a heart of worship, ready to be transformed.

Desires of Your Heart

I think this is one of God's favorite ways to communicate. He has far bigger plans for your life than you can imagine. If he told you what they are, you would be overwhelmed and perhaps filled with dread. He draws you toward his plan with a desire in your heart.

> **Delight** *yourself also in the LORD, And* **He shall give**
> **you the** **desires of your heart**. *(Psalm 37:4)*

God's plans for you are perfect and beautiful. The key to discovering them is to delight yourself in the Lord. Enjoy his company. Love up on him. Take pleasure in his presence. Soon, your desires may shift in a new direction. Let God lead you with your heart's desires.

Let Peace Reign

> *And **let the <u>peace of God rule</u>** in your hearts, ...*
> *(Colossians 3:15a)*

This little snip of scripture holds a grand revelation on receiving direction for making choices. The Greek word translated as *rule* means to *arbitrate, umpire,* or *govern.* Let the peace of God be the umpire of your internal debates. Choose the option that carries the most peace.

In this example, it was a warm blanket. I'm a facilitator and teacher by nature, not a writer. But I knew any path my ministry took would involve writing something. For weeks I searched for Christian writer's training and couldn't get comfortable with any options. Finally, a link popped up for a Christian women writers' group called Flourish Writers.

Tears streamed down my face as I watched the five-minute video on their homepage. The tangible peace of God wrapped its warmth and comfort around me. This group was where I belonged. My experience was dramatic. Most of the time, peace rules quietly. It makes you smile to know you heard from God. You won't wonder if you made the right choice. You'll move forward, confident you're where God wants you.

The Audible (to You) Voice Behind You

> ***<u>Your ears</u> shall hear a word <u>behind</u> you,** saying, "<u>This is the way, walk in it</u>," Whenever you turn to the right hand Or whenever you turn to the left. (Isaiah 30:21)*

Hearing God audibly in your head is rare. I believe he uses this method to communicate a warning of danger or when the fulfillment of his message will be delayed. It's as though he's behind you, speaking into your ear. They're essential words just for you and your situation. You may think there's someone talking behind you. But there isn't.

My best example of this phenomenon was when God called me into the ministry. I followed along in the bulletin as the associate pastor reviewed the church announcements. Suddenly, someone spoke boldly from behind my left ear. "Declare me before the nations," he said with authority. It was a command.

Confused and startled, I turned around to see who was there. But the lady in the row behind me just smiled and nodded her greeting. I heard from God that day.

Honor His Communication—Write It Down

God admonished Habakkuk to record the revelation he received.

> *Then the LORD answered me and said: "**Write the vision And make it plain** on tablets, That **he may run who reads it**. (Habakkuk 2:2)*

The purpose was to make the message easy to read and portable so others far away could read it.

What God shares with you is important. It may not be a significant prophecy intended for a nation, but it's so essential for your life that God spoke it to your heart. Write it down; make it plain so you can read it later; and rejoice.

CHAPTER EIGHT

UNLOCK THE GATEWAY
TO INTIMACY

The most effective thing you can do to enhance your pursuit of an intimate relationship with God is to receive the baptism in the Holy Spirit. One of the first things Jesus told his disciples about the Holy Spirit was that he would "testify of me." (John 15:26.) The Holy Spirit is the one who knows exactly who God the Father and Jesus Christ are, what belongs to them, and what they mean for you. He's the one who shares the truth about them with you.

Being baptized in the Holy Spirit opens a wide gateway to a deep relationship with God. It paves the way for God's grace-realities to flow from his heart into your life. The baptism in the Holy Spirit empowers and equips believers to live a rich, abundant Christian life on earth. There's little wonder that the enemy stirs up controversy and confusion about it.

My friend, if you've been taught that the baptism in the Holy Spirit is evil, no longer available to believers, or unnecessary, please stay with me. You deserve to know about God's most powerful gift for you as a believer.

Head Knowledge is not Enough

Remember this passage from the previous chapter?

> *But as it is written: **"Eye has not seen, nor ear heard, Nor have entered into the heart of man** The things which God has prepared for those who love Him." But God has **revealed them to us through His Spirit.** For the Spirit searches all things, yes, **the deep things of God**. (1 Corinthians 2:9-10)*

The knowledge you receive through mental study and input from your five senses can't reveal the depth of God's *heart* for you. Only the Holy Spirit accesses the deep things of God and brings them to your understanding. Approaching God with only the power of your intellect and reasoning hinders his influence and guidance.

> *For to be **carnally minded** is **death**, but to be **spiritually minded** is **life and peace**. Because the carnal mind is **enmity** against God; for it is not subject to the law of God, nor indeed can be. (Romans 8:6-7)*

To be *carnally minded* means to navigate the circumstances of life using only human reasoning and physical senses. According to Romans 8:7, a message to believers, the carnal mind is God's *enemy*. Being spiritually minded is easier with the power of the Holy Spirit.

Jesus Needed the Baptism in the Holy Spirit

In the Bible, Jesus is called both the *Son of God* and the *Son of Man*.

*And the angel answered and said to her, "**The Holy Spirit will come upon you**, and the power of the Highest will overshadow you; therefore, also, that Holy One who is to be born will be **called the Son of God**.
(Luke 1:35)*

Mary conceived Jesus by the Holy Spirit. He was the Son of God in his *spirit*. Jesus, the human being, didn't need to be born again. As the Son of God, he was born right with God and holy. But in his body and his mind, he was the son of Mary, a human. Jesus was called the Son of Man in *his humanness*.

But he needed more than spiritual righteousness, human reasoning, and a physical body when it was time to launch his ministry on earth. He needed supernatural wisdom, guidance, and the miracle-working power of the Holy Spirit. So, he went to his cousin, John the Baptist.

*When all the people were baptized, it came to pass that Jesus also was baptized; and **while He prayed, the heaven was opened**. And the **Holy Spirit descended** in bodily form like a dove **upon Him**, and a*

> *voice came from heaven which said, "You are My*
> *beloved Son; in You I am well pleased."*
> *(Luke 3:21-22)*

I believe Jesus prayed for the wisdom and power to do the universe-altering job he was sent to accomplish. God's answer was the *anointing* of the Holy Spirit. Jesus didn't pay the price of sin as the Son of God on earth. He did it as the Son of Man, a spiritually righteous human baptized in the power of the Holy Spirit. (Mark 8:31)

Two Operations of the Holy Spirit

God's Life and Nature in You at the New Birth

When you made Jesus your Lord and received his victory over sin as your victory, the Spirit of God, operating as the Spirit of Christ, kicked your dead spirit out and moved in.

> *But you are not in the flesh but in the Spirit, if indeed*
> **the Spirit of God dwells in you.** *Now if anyone **does***
> **not have the <u>Spirit of Christ</u>, he is not His.**
> *(Romans 8:9)*

You are now one spirit with Christ (1 Corinthians 6:17). The Spirit of Christ dwells in you and makes you the righteousness and holiness of God. You are now redeemed and restored to life in your spirit. You will go to heaven when you die, and you can have a relationship with God if you want it.

Because you have the Spirit of Christ, you have everything the Holy Spirit is, has, and knows in your spirit. But walking in the deep things of God through intimacy with him requires a level of submission to him not everyone is willing to make. The baptism in the Holy Spirit is the gateway to the deep things of God and intimacy with him.

Let's see how this played out in the lives of Jesus' disciples.

Baptism in the Holy Spirit is Power for Life and Ministry

I believe the disciples were born again after Jesus rose from the grave. They were behind locked doors, hiding from the Jews, when the risen Lord appeared with them. The disciples already acknowledged Jesus as their Lord and saw that he had risen from the dead. These are the requirements for being saved in Romans 10:9-10. All they needed was to receive the Spirit of Christ, who was there with them in Jesus.

Just as God's Spirit breathed life into Adam, Christ's Spirit breathed spiritual life into the disciples.

> *So Jesus said to them again, "Peace be with you. <u>As My Father has sent Me</u>, **even so I send you**." When He had said this. **He <u>breathed</u> on them** and said to them, "**<u>Receive</u> the Holy Spirit**. (John 20:21-22 MEV)*

You don't have to agree with me here. I know there are many opinions about these verses. But Jesus did exactly what God did when he breathed his Spirit into Adam (Genesis 2:7). I believe the disciples gladly opened their hearts and received the Spirit of Christ when Jesus breathed on them. I think they were born again in that room that night.

Jesus also commissioned them to take the news of the Savior into the world like the Father had sent him to be the Savior. But he knew they didn't have the *power* to accomplish the mission. Later, before his ascension, he met with them in Jerusalem.

> *And being assembled together with them, He* ***commanded*** *them not to depart from Jerusalem, but to* ***wait for the Promise of the Father [the Holy Spirit]****, "which," He said, "you have heard from Me; for John truly baptized with water, but you shall be* ***baptized with the Holy Spirit*** *not many days from now." ... But* ***you shall*** ***receive power*** *when the Holy Spirit has come* ***upon*** *you; and* ***you shall be*** ***witnesses*** *to Me in Jerusalem, and in all Judea and Samaria, and to the end of the earth." (Acts 1:4-5,8)*

My friend, Jesus insisted the born-again disciples wait for the baptism in the Holy Spirit before they attempted to fulfill their calling. They needed the power and supernatural involvement of God in their lives. And so do you. Every Christian is called to be a witness for Jesus wherever they are. You and I need the power and wisdom of the Holy Spirit to function in what we are called to do.

Essential for Every Christian

The power of the baptism in the Holy Spirit isn't exclusive to ministry situations. God also wants to provide wisdom and guidance in the mundane things of everyday life.

I believe the power of the Holy Spirit is essential for living the Christian life in our world today. Peter and John showed how vital they thought the baptism in the Holy Spirit was when they followed up on the Samaritan believers.

Philip went to Samaria to preach the Gospel and minister healing and miracles. Many believed and were born again. Word of their salvation got back to the apostles in Jerusalem.

*Now when the apostles who were at Jerusalem heard that **Samaria had received the word of God**, they sent **Peter and John** to them, who, when they had come down, **prayed for them that they might receive the Holy Spirit**. For as yet He had fallen **upon none of them**. They had only been baptized in the name of the Lord Jesus [in water]. Then they laid hands on them, and **they received the Holy Spirit**. (Acts 8:14-17)*

News that Samaritans were saved and baptized in water probably shocked the church leaders in Jerusalem. Samaritans practiced a version of Judaism that was considered inferior and pagan. The Jerusalem church didn't expect Samaria to receive Jesus as Christ, so they sent Peter and John to check it out.

The big guns of the early church didn't just pat the Samaritans on their backs and celebrate their salvation with a potluck dinner. They didn't leave until they invited every new believer to receive the baptism in the Holy Spirit. They considered it essential for the Samaritan church.

I expect most of the Samaritan believers weren't called to the ministry. They were regular people with normal lives. But they lived in a world hostile to Christians with sin and empty religion all around. Peter and John knew how important it was to have all the Holy Spirit power they could get. And it's still important for Christians today.

Yes, you can have a relationship with God without the baptism in the Holy Spirit. But your understanding of who you are in Christ will be incomplete. The limits of your mental understanding will hinder your relationship with God. And your ability to share your faith effectively will be restricted. To break past these limits, I invite you to receive the baptism in the Holy Spirit.

You'll find more information and a prayer to receive the Holy Spirit on the page "Receive the Baptism in the Holy Spirit" at the back of this book.

CHAPTER NINE

PERSONAL MINISTRY OF THE HOLY SPIRIT

The Holy Spirit dwells in every believer in his ministry as the Spirit of Christ. He imparts righteousness to you, restoring you to a right standing with God. But there's much more he can impart when you choose to receive the baptism in the Holy Spirit. You may be aware that there are gifts of the Holy Spirit for use in the corporate setting. However, my focus here is his ministry in your personal life.

And I will pray the Father, and he shall give you **another Comforter**, *that he may* **abide** **with you** **forever;** *(John 14:16 KJV)*

Guidance and Counsel of the Holy Spirit

These are some common ways the Holy Spirit reveals his wisdom and guidance.

Comfort in the Challenges

My sister often says, "Life is what happens when you have other plans." It's the nature of the fallen world for things to break down, accidents to happen, and tragedy to strike. In Jesus, you are positioned to overcome each of them in victory (John 16:33). One of the jobs held by the Holy Spirit is to offer comfort and peace through the process of overcoming.

> *Blessed be the God and Father of our Lord Jesus Christ, the Father of mercies and **God of all comfort, who comforts us in all our tribulation**, that we may be able to comfort those who are in any trouble, with the comfort with which we ourselves are comforted by God. (2 Corinthians 1:3-4)*

Human comfort, especially from loving friends, is a blessing. But it can't deal with deep pain and grief. The comfort of the Holy Spirit heals and delivers. Human comfort is godly. But the comfort of the Holy Spirit releases peace in the trial and equips you to help others in similar situations. May the Holy Spirit always be your primary comfort resource.

He Teaches and Reminds

Jesus was the source of understanding for the disciples while still with them. He welcomed their questions and answered carefully. But they could be exasperatingly thick-headed—kind of like you and me. They tried to relate his words to their natural environment with mental reasoning. Jesus wanted them to get the spiritual truth. He wants you to get it, too.

*These things I have spoken to you while being present with you. **But the <u>Helper</u>, the Holy Spirit**, whom the Father will send in My name, **He will <u>teach you all things</u>**, and **bring to your <u>remembrance</u> all things <u>that I said</u> to you**. (John 14:25-26)*

It's the job of the Holy Spirit to draw back the veil of flesh and reveal the nature and heart of God in the Word. Even an atheist can discern the history of the church and identify what the Bible calls godly behavior. But only the Holy Spirit can show you the depth of God's grace and his longing for the lost. He'll teach you what can only be spiritually discerned.

The Holy Spirit also helps you remember what the Lord said in the Word. This is especially important in ministry situations or when you need specific guidance.

He Testifies about Jesus

Most Christians can't imagine the depth of grace they've inherited in the finished work of Jesus. There's more to be known and more grace to be received regardless of how close your relationship with God is. It's the Holy Spirit's pleasure to reveal what Jesus secured for you at the cross.

*But when the Helper comes, whom I shall send to you from the Father, **the Spirit of truth** who proceeds from the Father, **He will <u>testify of Me</u>**. (John 15:26)*

Throughout the Bible, the Holy Spirit shines a light on who you are and what you have in your union with Christ. Jesus' victory over sin is just the beginning. There's always more to be revealed. Read the Word with your heart open to the Holy Spirit, and he will reveal more and more. This is the revelation knowledge that transforms.

An example from my life occurred at an evangelist's meeting. The speaker taught from the Word that God's spiritual grace-realities are already in us because he is in us. We receive them into our lives by faith. It was like the roof came off the building. I believed God's grace was out there in the cosmos somewhere with him. Other people seemed to receive healing and deliverance, but I didn't know how to get him to do it for me. Now, with this revelation, the fire of truth consumed my unbelief. I was instantly free from my wrong doctrine when I believed the Word for what it said. The paradigm of my life shifted, and I was transformed.

He Guides You into All Truth and Shows You Things to Come

At their last supper together, Jesus told his disciples there was more to say, but they couldn't handle it without the Holy Spirit. All they had was their human reasoning power, which couldn't discern the deep things of God.

> *I still have many things to say to you, **but you cannot bear them now**. However, **when He, the <u>Spirit of truth</u>, has come, He will <u>guide you into all truth</u>**; for He will not speak on His own authority, but **whatever He hears He will speak; and He will <u>tell you things to come</u>**. (John 16:12-13)*

My friend, mental reasoning is the *enemy* of God (Romans 8:6). Only the Holy Spirit can share *God's spiritual truth* with your heart. He does that through your relationship with God. You'll know which decision to make and which direction to go. He'll show you what to expect and warn you of trouble ahead. The Holy Spirit will be the guide you need.

He Glorifies Jesus in Your Life

As you receive the revelation of Jesus' victory, the Holy Spirit implements it in your life. Your close relationship with God is vital here. Staying full of God's life and keeping him in your thoughts give the Holy Spirit time to transform you. In the following passage, Jesus is still talking about the work of the Holy Spirit with his disciples. You can take this personally.

> *He will **glorify Me**, for He will **take of <u>what is Mine</u> and <u>declare</u> it to you**. <u>All things</u> that the Father has **are Mine**. Therefore I said that He will take of Mine and declare it to you. (John 16:14-15).*

I am filled with the life in these words! This speaks of the faith-bearing revelation of God's living, active, doing-it Word. Let's unwrap these verses.

What is mine: What belongs to Jesus? The abundant life he won for us does. That includes forgiveness of sin, healing, prosperity, wisdom, peace, love, joy, sound minds, healthy relationships, and everything you need for life and godliness. There is nothing you face or need that Jesus left out of the atonement.

Declare it to you: The Greek word translated as *declare* means *bring back word, announce truth,* or *report.*

When I let this soak in, I see the Holy Spirit take hold of what belongs to Jesus that you need. I see him instantly extend that grace-reality toward you. I see him point his holy finger at you and say with great force, "THIS IS YOURS!" And I see you receive it by faith, transform into its victory, and walk free at last.

Oh, my friend. This is the gospel of grace. You won't need God's grace in heaven; you need it now. As you grow more intimate with him, you will transform, not by your willpower, but by the revelation of the Holy Spirit.

The Gift of Tongues, Your Personal Prayer Language

The ability to pray in tongues is the unsung hero of the baptism in the Holy Spirit. With it, you speak God's language, bypassing the limitations of the human mind. With it, you unconditionally welcome his goodness into your life.

Paul said,

> *I thank my God **I speak with tongues <u>more than you all; yet in the church</u>** <u>I would rather speak five words with my understanding</u>, that I may teach others also, than ten thousand words in a tongue.*
> *(1 Corinthians 14:18-19)*

Yet in the church indicates Paul privately speaks in tongues more than you all. The everyday use of tongues is as a personal prayer language. See what Jude has to say about it.

> *But you, beloved,* **building yourselves** *up* **on** *your* **most holy faith, praying in the Holy Spirit,** *keep* **yourselves** *in the* **love of God,** *looking for the mercy of our Lord Jesus Christ unto eternal life. (Jude 20-21)*

In this passage, praying in the Holy Spirit refers to praying in tongues. You use your *most holy faith* to pray in tongues. Praying in the Spirit doesn't build up *your* faith. It uses God's faith, which you received when you were born again. Praying in the Spirit builds up *yourself.* Your *self* is your soul – your mind, will, emotions, and personality. It draws your soul into the influence of the Holy Spirit. Praying or speaking in tongues softens your heart so you can receive God's revelation, direction, and wisdom more easily. Moreover, it keeps you squarely in the ocean of God's love, where grace and mercy abide.

Praying in Tongues Prays the Perfect Will of God

> *Likewise,* **the Spirit helps us in our weaknesses,** *for* **we do not know what to pray for as we ought,** *but* **the Spirit Himself** *intercedes for us with groanings too deep for words. He who searches the hearts knows what the mind of the Spirit is, because* **He intercedes for the saints** **according to the will of God.** *(Romans 8:26-27 MEV)*

The Holy Spirit always prays the will of God in every situation. Yes, pray in your native language when others need to agree with you. Otherwise, use your personal prayer language to pray the perfect will of God. Pray in tongues.

Power for Personal Ministry

Every Christian is called to be a witness of Jesus and a minister of grace. Not all are called to a pulpit, but all are called to minister within arm's reach. The *power* of the Holy Spirit through the benefits we've covered yields great rewards when used in personal ministry to others.

Minister by example

Let the compassion of God lead the way when the Holy Spirit draws your attention to someone near you. A kind word, a door opened for someone with their arms full, or "Are you okay?" could open a transforming conversation.

Minister by divine encounter

I had a doctor's appointment one day. Her office was located about thirty minutes up the highway. God's glory moved into the car as I sang in the Spirit. My heart filled with joy, and compassion rose in me. I said, "Lord, let's minister together today. May I have a divine encounter along the way."

As I approached the entrance of her building, a young man, lost in thought, headed for the same door. We were about to bump into each other, so I slowed down to let him go ahead. "Oh, excuse me," he said. "Let me get the door." He was a little shorter than I, in his 30s, maybe. I noticed his curly brown hair and weathered countenance as he held the door. He caught up with me in the long, wide corridor and began to talk.

It was a story of betrayal and alimony, drugs and failure, dashed dreams and little hope. There was nothing I could say or do but nod and listen. I slowed down as we approached the elevator and said, "I'm headed up."

"I'm headed for the lab," he replied and crossed to pass before me. Just as he did, he stopped and turned. Looking into my eyes, he said, "My name is Luke. Will you pray for me?"

My dear friend. Only the Holy Spirit can set up a rendezvous like this. Only my boldness in the anointing of the Holy Spirit would move my hand to Luke's shoulder in the crowd around us. You bet I prayed for him and still do.

As you can see, baptism in the Holy Spirit makes his power and wisdom available in your everyday life and personal ministry. The benefits of the ministry of the Holy Spirit are essential for fulfilling the abundant Christian life God wants you to have. They flow to you through your intimate relationship with him.

CHAPTER TEN

THE CHOICE IS YOURS

Y ou can be sure. God wants you to know him as intimately as the limits of your flesh will allow. His great desire is for the flood of his grace to lavish you with abundant life. It's the love you give him that's the controlling factor. His love for you is already perfect and complete. So, God's first and great command gets right to the point.

> *Jesus said to him, "'You shall **love the LORD your God with all your heart**, with **all your soul**, and with **all your mind**.' This is the first and great commandment. (Matthew 22:37-38)*

You Must Choose

By default, you live life by human reasoning and your five senses. If you want to live guided by your relationship with God, you must choose and pursue that path.

After laying out the law in Deuteronomy, God gave the Hebrew people the bottom line.

I call heaven and earth as witnesses today against you, ***that I have set before you life and death, blessing and cursing; therefore*** <u>***choose life***</u>*, that both you and your descendants may live; (Deuteronomy 30:19 MEV)*

Thank God Jesus fulfilled the law by paying the price for all sin. But life and death are still a choice to make. God is all in with you. Are you all in with him?

The Enemy Wants to Thwart You

Satan, the enemy, doesn't care if you pray, read your Bible, or serve in the church as long as you're weak in your relationship with God.

Be sober, be vigilant; because ***your*** <u>***adversary***</u> ***the devil walks about*** <u>***like***</u> ***a*** <u>***roaring lion,***</u> ***seeking whom he*** <u>***may devour***</u>*. (1 Peter 5:8)*

The devil will devour the weak ones. He gets them off course with a few fiery darts. Mark 4:19 calls them the cares of this world, the deceitfulness of riches, and other desires. Fiery darts choke the Word, rendering it ineffective in the weak Christian's life. But not so in the lives of those who diligently seek God.

> *But <u>without faith it is impossible to please Him</u>, for **he***
> ***who comes to God must believe that He is, and that***
> ***He is a <u>rewarder</u> of those who <u>diligently seek Him</u>.***
> *(Hebrews 11:6 MEV)*

It takes faith to pursue a deeper relationship with God. So, believe the Word. God *rewards* those who diligently seek him! Meet him with faith. Yes, you'll annoy the enemy. But which do you prefer, the fiery darts or the rewards of those who pursue God?

God's Purpose is for You to Know Him

Do you remember the definition of eternal life from chapter one?

> *And **this is <u>eternal life</u>**, that **they may <u>know</u> You**, the*
> *only true God, and Jesus Christ whom You have sent.*
> *(John 17:3)*

God's purpose for salvation isn't so you can catch the train to heaven. It's so you can *know* him, the only true God, and his son Jesus eternally, including while you're on earth. He wants to show you his love *now* and always.

Start from Where You Are

Listen, God doesn't care how messy you are or how little progress you've made. No matter how close you are to him

today, he wants you to know him better. Ultimately, God
wants you to know him as well as he knows you.

> *For now <u>we see in a mirror, dimly,</u> but **then face to
> face.** <u>Now I know in part,</u> but **then <u>I shall know</u> just as
> <u>I also am known</u>.** (1 Corinthians 13:12 MEV)*

You will know God the way he knows you the instant you
meet him in glory. And you can start right now. He beckons
and draws you. He woos you with love. Turn and take one
step toward him. He will draw you the rest of the way.

> *But we all, with **unveiled face,** beholding as in a
> mirror <u>the glory of the Lord,</u> are **<u>being transformed</u>
> into the <u>same image</u> from glory to glory,** just as **by the
> Spirit of the Lord.** (2 Corinthians 3:18)*

Transformed, you will soon be overwhelmed with bliss as
you entwine your heart in him.
The choice is yours.

CHAPTER ELEVEN

HOW TO APPROACH GOD FOR INTIMACY

My friend, God wants more than an occasional encounter or mountaintop experience with you. He desires a sustained, continuing unity-of-heart relationship, as deep and intimate as you allow. That may be a place you've never been with him. The path begins in your daily prime time.

You may need to change your expectations as you enter his presence. Leave your troubles and needs at the door for now. Come in as though you belong there as a well-loved family member. Expect to be nourished at the table of God's Word. Expect to have a loving conversation as he reveals his heart to you.

*Your **words were found, and I ate them**, And **Your word was to me the joy and rejoicing of my heart;** For **I am called by Your name**, O LORD God of hosts. (Jeremiah 15:16)*

If you are ready to take your relationship with God to the next level, let's get started.

Pursue Friendship with God

Most Christians deeply respect God but don't consider him a dear friend. Yet that's exactly what he longs for. So, how do you pursue a loving friendship with God? Well, it's the same way you pursue friendship with anyone. You set up a meeting in a place conducive to a discussion, show up on time, and stay in their conversation. You don't make the meeting all about you.

Find a Good Time

I won't sugarcoat this. It takes time to cultivate an intimate relationship. A casual friendship can survive on conversations over lunch a few times a year. A close one can't. A good friendship can grow with a few minutes of contact per day. An intimate one can't. It takes regular, unhurried time to nurture an intimate relationship, including one with God.

There's no judgment here. If all you have is fifteen minutes, start there. God responds to what you can give him. Even so, I encourage you to look at your schedule for ways to give priority to relaxed meetings with God. Let him take you to new places in the Spirit and expect to linger there if that's what he wants.

Find Your Secret Place of Privacy

Your secret place is your relationship with the Spirit of God. As we covered earlier, you connect your soul with the spiritual realm by turning your thoughts, imagination, and attention to spiritual things. But your soul is easily distracted by intruding sights and sounds. Removing the distractions helps you keep your focus on God.

A private location at home or work where you can speak freely with God is ideal. I use my home office with the door shut. A friend prays in her car on the way to work. She arrives an hour before her coworkers to read the Bible. A pastor I know uses a closet. Privacy may not be too critical when building human friendships over lunch. But it's a great help when you want to share your heart with God.

Talk Directly to God

When you nurture a relationship with someone, you talk directly with them. You don't talk to their friends about them. That yields information about the *friend's* relationship and does nothing to promote yours. Your relationship with God deserves personal communication.

I don't have anything against good devotionals or books by Christian authors. But you only build intimacy with God through conversations with *him*. Talk directly to him. Read his words in the Bible. Use devotionals, books, and messages by others to inspire your face-to-face pursuit of intimacy with God, not instead of it.

Set the Tone

Make your meeting with God all about nurturing your relationship with him. Honor his desire for intimacy by removing deterrents to its pursuit.

Set aside your prayer list. When did you last meet your best friend for lunch and immediately give them a to-do list?

"Hi, Jack. It's great to see you. Listen, I need a new job. Can you find one for me today? Oh, and we had some storm damage last week. I know you'll have $500 in my account shortly. Nice seeing you. Bye."

Listen, God is ready to hear your prayer list. But there's no opportunity to build a love-based relationship with him if that's all he hears from you. Put your prayer list aside for a different meeting with God. Make your prime time all about getting to know him.

Calm distractions and establish boundaries. Your enemy, the devil, hates that you want to pursue God and not him. So, he will pull every trick he can to throw you off your plan. Your family will interrupt you. The phone will ring. Notifications will divert you. You'll think of twenty things you need to do all at the same time. I know the frustration. It's up to you to enforce the privacy you and the Lord need for relationship-building.

Put boundaries in place to guard your prime time:
- Use a space with a door that closes or pick a time when everyone else is asleep.
- Put the phone on do-not-disturb or turn it off.
- Keep a to-do list handy if a thought continues to nag.
- Train the family to interrupt only if there's blood or fire.
- Have what you need with you before you start.

Your time with God should be the most life-giving part of your day. Make potential interruptions and distractions wait outside until you're finished.

Use background worship tones. Lyric-free Christian worship tones can usher in a sense of peace during your prime time. Keep the volume low and use something that doesn't make you want to sing along. Let it support a worshipful attitude.

Establish a Prime Time Routine

Before I began to pursue God in earnest, my routine for prime time was self-serving. I apologized for being away from him for so long, whined about what was going on in my life, read a few verses of Scripture that fell flat, and begged him to fix my life. It was useless for much more than venting. But I didn't know what else to do.

I finally saw some progress when I found a set of spiritual exercises in a Bible study workbook. Over time, it transformed into the effective plan I use today. It's basically "pray and read the Bible" in a way that draws you close and opens your heart to hear God better. Here are the four steps that I use. Try them for yourself. I pray they help open your heart to God's love, acceptance, and grace.

Step 1: Enter His Presence. Enjoy His company.

You are a *spiritual* being. You must meet God in the Spirit to get to know him. You already know how. You do it every time you enter worship.

Fix your soul's attention on God and spiritual things. *Ling*er there with him.

> For those who **live according to the flesh <u>set their</u> <u>minds</u> on the things of the <u>flesh</u>**, *but those who* **live** *according to the Spirit, [<u>set their minds on</u>] the things of the <u>Spirit</u>. (Romans 8:5)*

You automatically have God's attention because you're born again. But there's no way to deepen your relationship with him unless he has yours. Turn your thoughts and imagination to the Lord and his spiritual environment.

Watch out. The devil wants to distract you. The more determined you are to pursue intimacy with God, the more the devil hates it. He will remind you of your negative self-talk and try to distract you. Don't let him.

> Therefore <u>**submit to God. Resist the devil**</u> **and he will** <u>**flee from you.**</u> **Draw near to God and He will draw near to you.** ... *(James 4:7-8a)*

Don't be wishy-washy about it, either. Resisting the devil *is* submitting to God. It draws you nearer. Here's a prayer you can pray out loud as you begin your prime time. Pray loud enough for your ears to hear it.

"Father, thank you for being here when I come. I push aside the distractions and thoughts of the day ahead and focus only on you. I gather up my cares and cast them on you. I resist the devil's distractions and negative thoughts. I receive only the thoughts and images you form in me."

Use your arms as you push away trouble and distractions. Make it real. Picture yourself entering his presence. Set your thoughts and imagination on him. Hang out there and linger in his love.

You are now *in the Spirit* with God.

Step 2: Entwine your Heart in Him. Enter worship.

God's love for you is as rich, complete, and holy as he is. God is pure, unconditional, unabashed love. He lives to flood your life with it. Love has a fantastic property; it expands the more it's given away. God expands your love for your family and others to match your love for him. Give all your love to God.

Set your love on him. Share your gratitude. Linger with him. Pray in the Spirit.

> *"Because he has **set his love** upon Me, therefore I will deliver him; I will set him on high, because **he has known My name**. (Psalm 91:14)*

When you stubbornly fix your love on God, it jams open the floodgates of his goodness. It blesses him to the core. But it's your choice to do that. Gratitude convinces you that you made the right choice. So, stop here for a few minutes. Get your Bible and read David's gratitude list in Psalm 103:1-22. … I'll wait.

Now, make a gratitude list of your own. How has God shown you mercy? How has he blessed you in nature, in family, in work? Tell him. Here's a sample prayer from my life. Replace my gratitude list with yours. Remember to pray out loud so your ears can hear the words.

"Father, I gather all my love and fix it on you. I entwine my heart in yours. You've proved your love for me over and over. You paid for my sin and set me free from hell forever. You put the things I shop for on sale before I get to the store. And I love how you clear the highway when I merge into traffic. I'm amazed and humbled by your goodness in my life. Thank you, Lord."

Pray in the Spirit. This is a great time to pray your love for God *in the Spirit*. The Holy Spirit uses your prayer language to pray your love perfectly.

Step 3: Engage the Word

Now, you're ready to open the Word of God. You're connected to him in the Spirit, and he'll reveal himself to you through his Word, the Bible.

> *In the beginning was the Word, and **the Word was with God**, and **the <u>Word was God</u>**. And **the Word became flesh** and dwelt among us, and we beheld His glory, the glory as of the only begotten of the Father, **full of grace and truth**. (John 1:1, 14)*

God and his Word are one. You can know the words of the Scriptures without knowing God. But you can't know God without the revelation of his heart through the Scriptures.

Read the Word out loud and slowly. The Bible is easier to understand than you think when you read it while in the Spirit. One of the jobs assigned to the Holy Spirit is to reveal the truth of the Scriptures. But you must let him communicate with your mind. So, read the words out loud and slowly. God will bring life and depth to his message. Stop and let the revelation soak in when he highlights a word or phrase. Look up the meanings of words that stand out. Write down what you learned and what it means for your life. Take the time to imagine what your life would be like if you implemented his message.

Have a reading plan in the New Testament. God dealt with humanity in the Old Testament differently from how he deals with us today. Back then, people were stuck in sin and rebellion with no way out. Punishment was appropriate for disobedience. Now that Jesus has paid the price for all sin, abundant grace through faith is how God interacts with us today. So, I suggest you read in the New Testament for a while. You'll get to know God as he works in you through Jesus.

Here's my suggested reading plan. I encourage you to start in the gospel of John. Then, read Acts through Revelation, then Matthew through Luke. When you finish, start over and do it again. The Lord will tell you when to include the Old Testament in your reading plan. Cover no more than a chapter a day. There's no rush. Start this step with prayer. Remember to pray out loud.

"Father, I engage you in your Word today. I submit myself to the revelation of who you are. I embrace your

life and your wisdom and receive your spirit-revealed
truth."

Step 4: Esteem His Revelation. Write it Down.

Honor God's faithfulness and take notes every time you
visit with him. Find a notebook or journal you'll enjoy using.
Note the date and any information you want to record as you
begin. You intend this to be a love-building time, so keep it
focused on knowing God better. Give him a chance to speak.
When he does, write down what he says.

"Father, thank you for my friend taking the first step
toward a closer relationship with you. May you reveal
your love and delight over them in ways that cannot be
denied. May they experience the depth of your love and
mercy that answers every doubt and fills them with joy.
In Jesus' name, amen."

Prime Time Resources

There's no better way to get to know God than through his revelation in the Word. Indeed, it is the only way. Jesus, the manifest Word of God, never stops revealing his father's heart.

> **The Son is the _dazzling radiance_ of God's splendor, the _exact expression_ of God's _true nature_—his mirror image!** *He holds the universe together and expands it by the mighty power of his spoken word. He accomplished for us the complete cleansing of sins, and then took his seat on the highest throne at the right hand of the majestic One. (Hebrews 1:3 TPT)*

Devotionals, books, and Bible studies offer insight and encouragement. But there is nothing like receiving truth and understanding by the revelation of the Holy Spirit. Give him a chance to "guide you into all truth." (See John 16:13.) Let him speak directly to your heart.

Study the Word of God. Renew Your Mind to God's Truth

The Holy Spirit is the only trustworthy teacher there is. Yes, seek insight from the great pastors and teachers of the Word. And confirm it by digging into the Word yourself. Use an accurate translation of the Bible. Find online or physical research resources. Use Hebrew and Greek dictionaries. And be quick to say "Yes, Lord" to the truth that exposes powerless religious traditions. Don't be afraid of the freedom of God's grace.

Prime Time Starter Kit

It doesn't take much preparation to meet with God. You, your Bible, a piece of paper, and a pen are plenty. However, you may want to upgrade your equipment as your relationship deepens. Here are my suggestions.

Get a Good Study Bible

Whatever Bible you have on hand is a great place to start. If it isn't a study-oriented Bible, I suggest you look for one. Most Bibles have a list of related scriptures for nearly all the verses. A study Bible has that plus much more. It may have maps, a concordance, original language definitions, detailed footnotes, or other valuable study resources along with the scriptures. There are many to choose from.

Use an Accurate Bible Translation. I encourage you to use an accurate translation rather than a paraphrase or common language version as your *study* Bible. The fullness of the original languages can be diluted by simple wording. Here are my suggestions:

Study Bible Translations: King James (KJV), New King James (NKJV), and Modern English Version (MEV). My study Bible is the *NKJV Spirit-Filled Life Bible*, published by Thomas Nelson.

Reference Translations: The Passion Translation (TPT), New Living Translation (NLT), and the Amplified Bible (AMP).

Study Aids

I use a variety of study aids and commentaries online, on my phone, and in print. Here are the ones I rely on every day:

Strong's Concordance: Every Christian serious about a deeper relationship with God needs this resource. It's an exhaustive English concordance of the King James Version of the Bible. Every word in the Bible is linked to the word it was translated from, Hebrew for Old Testament words or Greek for New Testament words. The Strong's Concordance dictionaries help you see the original meanings of the words in the KJV Bible.

Through this resource, God can speak to your heart to reveal a deeper understanding of his intent. It's available in print from online resources and Christian bookstores. Some online Bible apps make it available as well.

Living Commentary: *The Living Commentary* is an online and mobile app by Andrew Wommack Ministries. It contains his footnotes and commentary for over 27,000 of the 31,000 verses in the Bible. It also includes an interface to *Strong's Concordance* and other research resources. *The Living Commentary* is available from the Andrew Wommack Ministries online store.

Online Bible apps: There are many good Bible apps. I have two favorites.

The *Life Bible* app (lifebible.com) has an easy-to-use search feature, and verses copy beautifully to other documents. It has The Passion Translation Bible, which isn't carried by most other Bible apps.

The *Bible Hub* app (biblehub.com) is excellent for comparing translations and accessing Strong's Concordance.

Note-taking Supplies

You'll want to remember what God shares with you in your prime time. Keep his words safe and organized so you can find them later or share them with someone.

Physical Journal or Notebook: Select a notebook that suits your style and preferences. Mine is a blank, lined, spiral-bound notebook I found online. Over time, you'll determine how you like to organize yours.

Embellishment Supplies: Your prime time notebook is your private space. Spruce it up any way you like. I use highlighters, colored pens, and little stick-on tabs to mark my favorite entries. Other people may doodle, draw pictures, use watercolor paints, or glue in keepsakes.

Digital Notebook: A notebook app offers a way that's organized and searchable to capture thoughts, emails, posts, pictures, links, and comments. You may want to save what you learn from the Lord for future reference or sharing as your relationship with him grows. A digital notebook like OneNote or Evernote could be the solution.

Worship Tones

There are many resources for background worship tones available online. My favorite is *Moments of Worship* on YouTube.

Prime Time Guide

Step 1:   **Enter His Presence**
Set your mind on spiritual things.
Rid your thoughts of distractions.
Linger with him in the heavenly realms.
Enjoy his company.

Step 2:   **Entwine Your Heart in Him**
Set your love on God.
Express gratitude for the loving things he's
done in your life. Tell him how he's blessed
you. Meet with him in worship. Linger with
him. *Pray in the Spirit.*

Step 3:   **Engage the Word of God**
God and his Word are one.
Pray for revelation. Read the Word out loud.
Ponder his revelations. Give him time to
speak.

Step 4:   **Esteem His Revelation**
Write down what God shows you.
Note the date and the scriptures you read.
Research special scriptures.
Record your responses and how your life is
affected by his revelations.

Be Born Again

To have a real relationship with God, you must be born again. Jesus began a conversation with Nicodemus, a Pharisee, with this right-to-the-point statement:

> *Jesus answered and said to him, "Most assuredly, I say to you,* **unless one is born again, he <u>cannot</u> see the kingdom of God.***" (John 3:3 MEV)*

And to his disciples at the last supper before his crucifixion, he said:

> *Jesus said to him, "****I am the way****, the truth, and the life.* ***No one comes to the Father <u>except through Me</u>****."* *(John 14:6 MEV)*

The decision to put your trust in Jesus is the best one you will ever make. There are no hoops to jump through. There's no need to clean up your act first. Jesus paid the price for all sin for all people for all time by his loving grace. You receive it done for you by faith.

> *... that if you* **confess with your mouth <u>the Lord Jesus</u> and believe in your heart that <u>God has raised Him from the dead</u>, <u>you will be saved</u>***. ... For whoever calls on the name of the LORD shall be saved.* *(Romans 10:9-10, 13)*

Pray this prayer aloud.

"God, thank you for sending Jesus to pay for my sins with his life. I confess that he alone is my Lord and my Savior. I believe in my heart you raised him from the dead. Now, I receive his life and righteousness. Thank you, Jesus, for saving me!"

Congratulations, my friend. You are heaven-bound! A great resource to start you on your journey with the Lord is the book *The New You & The Holy Spirit* (Wommack 2008).[4] It's available from online bookstores or his website, www.awmi.net.

Receive the
Baptism in the Holy Spirit

God is eager to give you the supernatural power to live a victorious Christian life. You receive that power through the baptism in the Holy Spirit. No born-again person is excluded from this offer.

> *If you then, being evil, know how to give good gifts to your children,* ***how much more*** *will your heavenly Father* ***give the Holy Spirit to those who ask Him****!*
> *(Luke 11:13)*

All you need to do is ask in faith and receive the Holy Spirit.

Pray this prayer out loud.

"Father, I'm so grateful that you saved me. I want all you have for me and the power to live it out. Please baptize me in the Holy Spirit. I receive him now. I receive his power. Holy Spirit, I embrace you and rejoice that you are in my life!"

Congratulations, friend. You received the baptism in the Holy Spirit. You also received your heavenly prayer language. It bypasses the limits of your mind and enables you to pray and praise God perfectly using the power of the Holy Spirit. This is called praying in tongues.

Begin to praise God out loud but not in a known language. Let the Holy Spirit form heavenly words as you speak forth syllables from your heart by faith. As you speak, the Holy

Spirit releases precisely what you need from the well of his grace.

Notes

1. *Strong's Concordance* and *Strong's Lexicon* are the resources used for all definitions and explanations of Hebrew and Greek words in Scripture. These resources are accessed through https://biblehub.com/ by entering the Bible verse and selecting the *Strong's* option. The word being defined or explained is found and the Strong's Greek or Hebrew reference number is selected. The resulting webpage contains explanation and usage information from Strong's Lexicon and definitions from Strong's Concordance.

   Strong's resources are provided by: *Thayers Greek Lexicon*, Electronic Database. Copyright © 2002, 2003, 2006, 2011 by Biblesoft, Inc. All rights reserved. Used by permission. BibleSoft.com and
   Brown-Driver-Briggs Hebrew and English Lexicon, Unabridged, Electronic Database. Copyright © 2002, 2003, 2006 by Biblesoft, Inc. All rights reserved. Used by permission. BibleSoft.com.

2. *Oxford English Dictionary*: www.oed.com.

3. *Cambridge Dictionary*: dictionary.cambridge.org.

4. Wommack, Andrew. *The New You & The Holy Spirit*. Colorado Springs. Andrew Wommack Ministries Inc. 2008.

About the Author

Sharon Deming was born to teach and mentor. At age six, she led a first grade reading group and never quit mentoring. Whatever she values, she lives and teaches. Her master's degree in counseling and her degree from Charis Bible College equip her to share what she values most—the living Word of God and how to nurture intimacy with him. Her monthly email journal, *Hearts Entwined in Him*, offers Word-based inspiration and insight toward a deeper relationship with God.

You can find me at sharondeming.com.

SHARONDEMING.COM